I'VE BEEN THINKING . . .

THE JOURNAL

ALSO BY MARIA SHRIVER

I've Been Thinking . . .

And One More Thing Before You Go . . .

Ten Things I Wish I'd Known—Before I Went Out into the Real World

Just Who Will You Be?: Big Question. Little Book. Answer Within.

We Empower: Inspirational Wisdom for Women

What's Heaven?

What's Wrong with Timmy?

What's Happening to Grandpa?

Color Your Mind: A Coloring Book for Those with Alzheimer's and the People Who Love Them

The Shriver Report: A Woman's Nation Pushes Back from the Brink

The Shriver Report: A Woman's Nation Changes Everything

The Shriver Report: A Woman's Nation Takes on Alzheimer's

THIS BOOK IS WRITTEN BY:

_____

Maria Shriver

I'VE BEEN THINKING . . .
THE JOURNAL

Inspirations, Prayers, and Reflections
for Your Meaningful Life

PAMELA DORMAN BOOKS · VIKING

VIKING
An imprint of Penguin Random House LLC
penguinrandomhouse.com

A Pamela Dorman Book/Viking

Excerpts from *The Story of Ruth: Twelve Moments in Every Woman's
Life (Eerdmans)* by Joan Chittister. Used by permission of Benetvision.

ISBN 9781984878021 (hardcover)

Printed in the United States of America
3   5   7   9   10   8   6   4   2

Book design by Meighan Cavanaugh

For Katherine, Christina, Patrick, and Christopher
I love you all to the moon and back.

And to all who have the courage to embark
on the quest for a meaningful life

Contents

I'VE BEEN THINKING . . .

THE JOURNAL

Introduction

Dear Friend,

As you open this new journal of yours, the first thing I want to do is thank you for having the courage to think about your own life. The fact that you even picked this up should tell you that you're already on the path to a meaningful life. You wouldn't be reading these words if you weren't. So, bravo!

The truth is, no matter our age, no matter our background, we all could use some guidance, wisdom, and inspiration to help us live a life that is uniquely our own. My book *I've Been Thinking . . .* was my attempt to share with you my own thoughts about a meaningful life. I hoped in doing so that it would get you thinking about what *you* value. About what you believe in. About what's really important to you. The response to the book was incredibly humbling, and along the way, many people asked if I would consider creating a journal where they could write their own thoughts as well. Well, voila! Here it is!

Writing has always been one of my most therapeutic tools. Time and again, it's helped me figure out what I'm thinking and feeling. It's also helped me get centered and get clear. In this journal, I wanted to give you the space and the encouragement to explore your own thoughts and feelings for yourself. I hope it helps you gain clarity and that it centers you on your path forward.

Throughout this journal, you'll find writing prompts inspired by the essays in *I've Been Thinking* . . . . There are inspirations for each week of the year. I've made this a weekly guide, because I myself sit down once a week to gather my thoughts and write.

My hope is that this journal will be a tool to help you make time each week to reflect on your life and write down what *you've* been thinking. You see, I believe that everyone is a writer, even if they don't think they are good at it. If you can think, then you can write. Your voice deserves to be heard as much as mine or anyone else's, so start using it here on these pages. (And if you need more inspiration, then pick up *I've Been Thinking* . . . , which has additional writing on all the topics covered here.)

In addition to providing space for you to respond to the writing prompts, I've also included additional space for you to reflect midweek and for you to write down your "yippee! moments" of the week as well. "Yippee! moments" are what I like to call any experience or encounter that made me smile or jump for joy. Sometimes those moments are big. Other times they're small. But trust me, even during our hardest weeks, there is *something* worth celebrating.

. . .

As with *I've Been Thinking . . .* , you can use this journal in whatever way suits you best. The essays are organized according to the seasons and holidays of the year, but feel free to jump around and respond to whatever inspires you in that moment. This is your journey and your journal. How you use it is up to you.

In addition to the weekly inspirations, you'll also find quotes and prayers to inspire you and make you think. In *I've Been Thinking . . .* , I wrote about how I use "Dear God" to start my prayers because those words reflect my faith and my beliefs. That said, I know that not everyone prays to the same God or uses that word. Some don't pray at all. That's why in this journal I've included my own prayers, and left space for you to write your own. That way you can fill in the blank however you'd like.

I've also included a "midyear check-in" within the pages of this journal. That's because I like to make a point of allotting time throughout the year to stop and take stock of how my life is going. Is my year going the way I expected it to go? If not, can I redirect myself to better serve my goals, hopes, and dreams? I like to ask myself these questions every few months so that I can evaluate where I am on the path of my life.

I'm so excited for you to start this process. I hope you'll dig deep in this journal, as I did when writing *I've Been Thinking . . . .* And, when you're done with your writing, I hope you'll be brave enough to share some of your words with others. That could just mean sharing an essay with someone you love. Or it could mean sharing it online with a community of other people seeking wisdom and inspiration. If you ever feel ready to share publicly, I invite you to visit my website at www.mariashriver.com/sunday paper/ and submit your essay to my team. We'll consider publishing it in a future edition of *The Sunday Paper* newsletter, which is where all of the essays in my book *I've Been Thinking . . .* originated.

So, off you go. Turn the page now and get started. I wish you all the best on your personal journey to a meaningful life.

With love,
Maria

Every morning, I start my day with this version of Saint Teresa's prayer. I included it at the beginning of *I've Been Thinking . . .* , and I wanted to include it again in this journal because I really do believe it's a great way to start things out. I hope it helps you. Enjoy.

May today there be peace within

May you trust God that you are exactly
where you are meant to be

May you not forget the infinite
possibilities that are born of faith

Maybe you use those gifts that you have
received and pass on the love that has been
given to you

May you be content knowing that
you are a child of God

Let this presence settle into your bones
and allow your soul the freedom
to sing, dance, praise, and love

It is there for each and every one of us.

—SAINT TERESA OF AVILA

What I'm Carrying with Me into the New Year

"I keep turning over new leaves, and spoiling them, as I used to spoil my copy-books; and I make so many beginnings there never will be an end."

—Laurie, in *Little Women* by Louisa May Alcott

A new year is always thrilling because we have the chance to make it our best one yet. At the beginning of each year, I like to make a list of all the things I want to leave behind. I also like to make a list of the positive things in my life that I want to carry forward. I encourage you to try this same exercise. As you enter this new year, ask yourself: What do I want to bury from my past, and what do I want to bring with me into the future? Also ask yourself: How do I define a meaningful life, and how do I want it to look for me? What steps do I need to take today to begin this journey?

_____

_____

_____

Dear God, living with regret and guilt for my past mistakes is a heavy burden to carry. Free me from the chains of remorse over things I've done that I wish I could do over. Please help me know in my heart that I can make a fresh start whenever I decide to. Free me to look ahead and not keep looking back. Amen

_Dear _____,_

MIDWEEK REFLECTION

How are things going for you this week, so far? What more can
you do this week to focus your intentions and move forward on
your path to a meaningful life?

_____

_____

_____

_____

_____

_____

MY YIPPEE! MOMENT OF THE WEEK . . .

What brought you joy or made you smile this week?

_____

_____

_____

_____

_____

_____

MY INTENTIONS FOR THE NEW YEAR . . .

(A little more space for you to reflect on your goals for this year.)

_____

_____

_____

_____

_____

_____

_____

_____

_____

_____

_____

_____

_____

_____

_____

_____

_____

I Am Who I Choose to Become

"What lies behind us and what lies before us are
tiny matters compared to what lies within us."

—attributed to Ralph Waldo Emerson

This quote that is attributed to Ralph Waldo Emerson
has always been one of my favorites because it tells me
that everything I need to get through life is within me.
It also reminds me not to waste too much time worrying about
what I can't control, and instead to focus my energy on the here
and now. So today, ask yourself: Do I really believe that I have
everything I need within me? If not, what am I missing and
what do I need?

_____

_____

_____

_____

_____

_____

_____

_____

_____

_____

_____

_____

_____

_____

_____

_____

_____

_____

_____

> *Dear God, I trust you will meet me right where I am. Help me to make choices that are good for me and those I love. Help me to become the person I'm meant to be. Help me to say and believe that today, I am enough and I am worthy. Help me to know that each day is a gift, and I can begin anew. Amen.*

Dear _____ ,

MIDWEEK REFLECTION

How are things going for you this week, so far? What more can you do this week to focus your intentions and move forward on your path to a meaningful life?

_____

_____

_____

_____

_____

_____

_____

MY YIPPEE! MOMENT OF THE WEEK . . .

What brought you joy or made you smile this week?

_____

_____

_____

_____

_____

_____

_____

WEEK 3

Bring Joy into Your Home

"There is no doubt in my mind that we could all use more 'yippee' moments in our lives. We could all use more laughter and more joy."

—Maria

Living a life of joy is critical, especially as we get older and unfunny things start to happen. I try to live my life with lightness and constantly remind myself not to take things too seriously. (This isn't always easy, but I think it's a good goal nonetheless.) This week, close your eyes, get quiet, and think about what brings you joy. What makes you feel light and free? Who and what makes you feel joyful, and how can you add more joy to your life each and every day?

_____

_____

_____

_____

_____

_____

_____

_____

_____

_____

Dear God, help me feel the joy in my own heart. Help me feel the joy that is around me. Help me be a messenger of joy in my family. Help me become a beacon of joy in the lives of others. Amen.

Dear _____ ,

MIDWEEK REFLECTION

How are things going for you this week, so far? What more can you do this week to focus your intentions and move forward on your path to a meaningful life?

_____

_____

_____

_____

_____

_____

_____

MY YIPPEE! MOMENT OF THE WEEK . . .

What brought you joy or made you smile this week?

_____

_____

_____

_____

_____

_____

The Power of Listening

"When people talk listen completely. . . . Most people never listen."

—Ernest Hemingway

Ibelieve that we all share a desire to be seen, to matter, to belong. We all want someone to listen to us because listening makes us feel heard and understood. Listening to those we love is truly an act of kindness because it proves to people that we care. How can you take more time to listen to the people who you love this week? What more can you do to let them know that they are heard? (As my daughter always says, "I don't need you to fix my problems . . . I just need you to listen.")

_____

_____

_____

_____

_____

_____

_____

_____

_____

_____

> *Dear God, I pray I will always have good friends around me and that we will influence, encourage, and inspire one another to be the best we can be. I pray for friends who will speak the truth out of love for me, give me sound counsel when I need it, and be of help in difficult times. Help me to be that kind of friend to them as well. Amen.*

Dear _____ ,

MIDWEEK REFLECTION

How are things going for you this week, so far? What more can you do this week to focus your intentions and move forward on your path to a meaningful life?

_____

_____

_____

_____

_____

_____

_____

MY YIPPEE! MOMENT OF THE WEEK . . .

What brought you joy or made you smile this week?

_____

_____

_____

_____

_____

_____

_____

The Power of Gratitude

"Gratitude is a flower that blooms in noble souls."

—Pope Francis

Every morning when I open my eyes, I thank God for the gift of life. I also give thanks for my health, my family, my friends, and for the country I'm blessed to live in. Having a gratitude practice like this one can not only change the course of your day, but it can change your entire life. Use this space this week to write about what you're most grateful for. Then, think about how you can bring those things into your daily life.

_____

_____

_____

_____

_____

_____

_____

_____

_____

_____

_____

_____

_____

_____

_____

_____

_____

_____

Dear God, thank you for all the times when I am blessed by the kindness of others. You have surrounded me with people who care for me and bless me every day with kind words and actions. Help me to show them the same kindness they have provided. Help me to know how deeply I appreciate them and to know that I treasure them as a gift from you to me. Amen.

Dear _____ ,

MIDWEEK REFLECTION

How are things going for you this week, so far? What more can you do this week to focus your intentions and move forward on your path to a meaningful life?

_____

_____

_____

_____

_____

_____

_____

MY YIPPEE! MOMENT OF THE WEEK . . .

What brought you joy or made you smile this week?

_____

_____

_____

_____

_____

_____

The Power of Peace Starts from Within

"If there is light in the soul, there will be beauty in the person. If there is beauty in the person, there will be harmony in the house. If there is harmony in the house, there will be order in the nation. If there is order in the nation, there will be peace in the world."

—Chinese proverb

I think we can all agree that we need more peace in our country and in the world. Over the years, though, I've come to learn that the peace we're all asking for actually starts within ourselves. It's not always easy to find peace, but it's critical that we try. So, this week, try focusing on your own inner peace. Try getting up a few minutes earlier each morning just to give yourself time to cultivate that peace. Then, write about what you feel and notice about how it affects your life.

_____

_____

_____

_____

_____

_____

_____

_____

_____

_____

_____

_____

_____

_____

> *Dear God, I am amazed at the greatness and majesty of all you have created. Thank you for how nature speaks to me of your great power and design. Thank you for the beauty of the flowers and the sunsets and the oceans and the mountains. Thank you for the peace in my own home. Amen.*

Dear _____ ,

MIDWEEK REFLECTION

How are things going for you this week, so far? What more can you do this week to focus your intentions and move forward on your path to a meaningful life?

_____

_____

_____

_____

_____

_____

MY YIPPEE! MOMENT OF THE WEEK . . .

What brought you joy or made you smile this week?

_____

_____

_____

_____

_____

_____

What I Learned About Power from a Community of Nuns

"The moment a woman comes home to herself, the moment she knows that she has become a person of influence, an artist of her life, a sculptor of her universe, a person with rights and responsibilities who is respected and recognized, the resurrection of the world begins."

—Sister Joan Chittister

Some of the most powerful women I've ever met have been nuns. Why? Well, I've thought quite a bit about this and I've come to realize that it's because their work aligns with their values and who they really are. Nuns work in community, they live in community, and they believe that they should use their lives and their work to support their community. I love that. This week, ask yourself: Does my work align with my beliefs? Does my professional life reflect my personal values? If not, what can I do to change that?

_____

_____

_____

_____

_____

_____

_____

_____

_____

_____

_____

_____

Dear God, as I move forward in life, help me to stay grounded in my values. Guide me toward those values and guide me toward a community where I will be supported and loved. Amen.

Dear _____ ,

MIDWEEK REFLECTION

How are things going for you this week, so far? What more can you do this week to focus your intentions and move forward on your path to a meaningful life?

_____

_____

_____

_____

_____

_____

_____

MY YIPPEE! MOMENT OF THE WEEK . . .

What brought you joy or made you smile this week?

_____

_____

_____

_____

_____

_____

_____

The Power of Positive Thinking

"What you're supposed to do when you don't like
a thing is change it. If you can't change it, change
the way you think about it."

—Maya Angelou

I spend a lot of time thinking, and lately I've been trying something new. Any time a negative thought arises in my mind, I try to think about how I can shift my perspective. This week, ask yourself how you can do the same. What can you do when a challenging or negative thought pops up in your mind? You have the power to reframe your thoughts at any point during the day or during your life. So, try doing it and notice how it makes you feel.

_____

_____

_____

_____

_____

_____

_____

_____

_____

_____

_____

_____

_____

_____

_____

Dear God, so many negative, critical thoughts and lies about myself and my circumstances have made their way into my mind. Help me to learn to silence those voices. Help me to speak the truth to lies and negativity and to fill my mind instead with what is good and beautiful about me and around me. Amen.

Dear _____ ,

MIDWEEK REFLECTION

How are things going for you this week, so far? What more can you do this week to focus your intentions and move forward on your path to a meaningful life?

_____

_____

_____

_____

_____

_____

_____

MY YIPPEE! MOMENT OF THE WEEK . . .

What brought you joy or made you smile this week?

_____

_____

_____

_____

_____

_____

The Power of Women

"No one can make you feel inferior without your consent."

—Eleanor Roosevelt

I was raised in a family of men, but I was also raised by a formidable mother who taught me to believe in the power of women. She reminded me that being a woman was my greatest asset, and that when women are seen and heard and validated, they can do anything. What unique assets do you feel that women bring to your life, your family, your workplace, and the world? How might you honor the matriarchs of your life and recognize them for their strength, their wisdom, and their life experiences? What does power mean to you?

_____

_____

_____

_____

_____

_____

_____

_____

_____

_____

_____

_____

_____

_____

_____

_____

_____

Dear God, thank you for the women who helped shape my life. Please bless each of them and enrich them for the way they influenced me. Help me to live their wisdom and strength. Help me continue to embrace your plan for my life and keep moving forward into the life you envision for me. Amen.

Dear _____ ,

MIDWEEK REFLECTION

How are things going for you this week, so far? What more can you do this week to focus your intentions and move forward on your path to a meaningful life?

_____

_____

_____

_____

_____

_____

_____

MY YIPPEE! MOMENT OF THE WEEK . . .

What brought you joy or made you smile this week?

_____

_____

_____

_____

_____

_____

_____

The Power of Family

"Bonding with loved ones is a great gift that feeds your spirit. It refreshes you and reminds you of what's ultimately important in life."

—Maria

I grew up in a big family—one that taught me a lot about connection, communication, loyalty, and love. My friends always remind me that not everybody is as close to their family as I am, but the reality is that we've all been shaped by our families in some way. And now, you get to decide what kind of family you want to have. We're each capable of creating the family that we want, so this week, think about how do you define family? Who do you want sitting at your kitchen table? What lessons do you want to carry from your childhood into the present, and what do you want to leave behind?

_____

_____

_____

_____

_____

_____

_____

_____

_____

_____

Dear God, with life as crazy busy as it is, I need to find ways to show my family they are more important to me than my work and other things that involve my time. Help me to plan one-on-one time with them. Help me to continue to forge more wonderful, new memories of sweet moments together. Amen.

Dear _____ ,

MIDWEEK REFLECTION

How are things going for you this week, so far? What more can you do this week to focus your intentions and move forward on your path to a meaningful life?

_____

_____

_____

_____

_____

_____

_____

MY YIPPEE! MOMENT OF THE WEEK . . .

What brought you joy or made you smile this week?

_____

_____

_____

_____

_____

_____

_____

What Is Love?

"The most important thing that I know about living is love. Nothing surpasses the benefits received by a human being who makes compassion and love the objective of his or her life. For it is only by compassion and love that anyone fulfills successfully their own life's journey. Nothing equals love."

—Sargent Shriver

There is love all around us. I didn't always know that, but it's true. Love shows itself to us in so many different ways, but we often miss the small acts of love because we're too caught up trying to search for the grand gestures that we've seen in films or read about in books. That's a shame because there is a love story going on around us in real time. So today, focus on the small acts of love all around you. What do you notice? Do you know what makes you feel loved? Make a list. Write it down.

_____

_____

_____

_____

_____

_____

_____

_____

_____

_____

_____

_____

_____

_____

Dear God, help me to acknowledge and to experience your gift of love. I know that you built this world from a place of love and that if I look for it, I will find love all around me. Even when I feel wounded or have a broken heart, I know you will remind me that I'm loved and that you will give me the courage to love again. Amen.

Dear _____ ,

MIDWEEK REFLECTION

How are things going for you this week, so far? What more can you do this week to focus your intentions and move forward on your path to a meaningful life?

_____

_____

_____

_____

_____

_____

_____

MY YIPPEE! MOMENT OF THE WEEK . . .

What brought you joy or made you smile this week?

_____

_____

_____

_____

_____

_____

The Power of Laughter

"One day we will look back on all this and laugh."

—Quite a few people over the years

Life can be challenging for all of us, but laughter is one of the best remedies I've found for letting the air out of any situation that feels heavy. This week, write down what makes you laugh. Write down the people in your life who you can count on for a laugh. (As my daughter always says, "Make sure you have at least one funny friend." She's so right.)

_____

_____

_____

_____

_____

_____

_____

_____

_____

_____

_____

_____

_____

_____

_____

_____

_____

_____

Dear God, thank you for the joy I have in my life. Thank you for the gift of laughter, how it lightens my heart. Help me to be a messenger of joy for others, and help me to laugh at myself. Amen.

Dear _____ ,

MIDWEEK REFLECTION

How are things going for you this week, so far? What more can you do this week to focus your intentions and move forward on your path to a meaningful life?

_____

_____

_____

_____

_____

_____

_____

MY YIPPEE! MOMENT OF THE WEEK . . .

What brought you joy or made you smile this week?

_____

_____

_____

_____

_____

_____

_____

Talk of Love, Not Hate

"Note to self: My words have impact. They can build someone up or tear them down. They can provide hope or create despair. Use them wisely. Use them to make someone's day, not ruin it."

—Maria

We live in a world where a lot of hateful words get tossed around. Sometimes others toss them at us. Sometimes our own inner voice throws them at us. The way we use our voice has a great effect on how we feel about ourselves and how we make others feel about themselves. This week, reflect on how can you use your voice to spread love in this world, instead of hate. How can you speak from a place of love and help cut down on the bullying that is so pervasive in our culture?

This week, I share with you the Prayer of Saint Francis. It's one I turn to quite frequently and, regardless of your religion, I think it offers good guidance for everyone who is seeking a meaningful life.

PRAYER OF SAINT FRANCIS

Lord, make me an instrument of your peace:
where there is hatred, let me sow love;
where there is injury, pardon;
where there is doubt, faith;
where there is despair, hope;
where there is darkness, light;
where there is sadness, joy.

O divine Master, grant that I may not so much seek
to be consoled as to console,
to be understood as to understand,
to be loved as to love.

For it is in giving that we receive,
it is in pardoning that we are pardoned,
and it is in dying that we are born to eternal life.
Amen.

*Dear*_____ ,

MIDWEEK REFLECTION

How are things going for you this week, so far? What more can you do this week to focus your intentions and move forward on your path to a meaningful life?

_____

_____

_____

_____

_____

_____

MY YIPPEE! MOMENT OF THE WEEK . . .

What brought you joy or made you smile this week?

_____

_____

_____

_____

_____

_____

The Power of Kindness

"Kindness is the language that the deaf can hear
and the blind can see."

—attributed to Mark Twain

We all want to be treated with kindness, because we're all struggling in some way. Treating others with kindness isn't always easy, though. It requires patience. It requires empathy. It requires you to be conscious of your words and actions. This week, think about kindness. What does it mean to you? Do you think about being kind in your everyday life? Could you be kinder? If you're struggling with kindness, write down why.

_____

_____

_____

_____

_____

_____

_____

_____

_____

_____

Dear God, thank you for the kindness, mercy, and generosity you show me every day, and I ask you to help me to see those around me in the same way—as people who are loved and treasured. Please make my heart as tender as yours, so that I may actively reach out and show kindness and a generous spirit to all the people in my life today. Amen.

Dear _____ ,

MIDWEEK REFLECTION

How are things going for you this week, so far? What more can you do this week to focus your intentions and move forward on your path to a meaningful life?

_____

_____

_____

_____

_____

_____

_____

MY YIPPEE! MOMENT OF THE WEEK . . .

What brought you joy or made you smile this week?

_____

_____

_____

_____

_____

_____

Why We Should Stop Trying to "Go It Alone"

"You have the power to awaken others to their potential, to help them see that they are not alone, and to challenge them to find inspiration in their own story."

—Maria

We're never going to move humanity forward if we think we can "go it alone." We all need each other, and we all need to be brave enough to ask for help. (This was, and still is, a challenge for me.) So this week, be brave enough to utter the words "I need help" or ask someone "Could you help me?" If you're struggling with that, ask yourself what you find hard about it. Write how you feel about asking for help.

_____

_____

_____

_____

_____

_____

_____

_____

Dear God, our culture exalts the outwardly strong, independent people who chart their own course, pave their own way, and "go it alone." But the truth is that no one really does anything alone, and to try is overwhelming, isolating, and exhausting. I struggle with weakness, shortcomings, and inadequacy, and yet I resist asking for help. Please teach me to humble myself and cultivate the practice of seeking help from others and from you. I open my heart to receiving and giving help, and I ask your forgiveness for those times I have tried to handle it all on my own. Amen.

Dear_____ ,

MIDWEEK REFLECTION

How are things going for you this week, so far? What more can you do this week to focus your intentions and move forward on your path to a meaningful life?

MY YIPPEE! MOMENT OF THE WEEK . . .

What brought you joy or made you smile this week?

Looking for the Light in the Cracks

"The most important thing in life is to learn how to give out love, and to let it come in."

—Morrie Schwartz

As the noise of the news continues to get louder, I have found myself trying to look for the spaces and places of quiet. I find myself looking for the light. We live in a confusing, chaotic world, but I believe that there is still a lot of good in our midst. It helps to open our eyes and look for it. This week, try to think of yourself as a light in this world. Who can you be a light for? Who brings light to your life?

_____

_____

_____

_____

_____

_____

_____

_____

_____

_____

_____

_____

_____

_____

_____

_____

Dear God, thank you that you are the God of love and that your love is the light that shines in this present darkness. May it shine into my heart and give me the strength and compassion to love others like you do. There is no weapon and no instrument for change on our planet more powerful than your love. Amen.

Dear _____ ,

MIDWEEK REFLECTION

How are things going for you this week, so far? What more can you do this week to focus your intentions and move forward on your path to a meaningful life?

_____

_____

_____

_____

_____

_____

_____

MY YIPPEE! MOMENT OF THE WEEK . . .

What brought you joy or made you smile this week?

_____

_____

_____

_____

_____

_____

_____

Easter Reflections

"He is not here. He has risen!"

—Luke 24:6

For me, Easter is a holiday that's all about rising. (I'm not just talking about Jesus rising from the dead, although that's my metaphor.) I believe that it can serve as a meaningful reminder that each of us has the opportunity to rise to the occasion that is our life. This week, think about how you can rise in your life. How can you rise above any problems and challenges that you may be facing? If you're having a tough week, pause and realize that you can rise, no matter how difficult the present situation is. Use this space to write about what you want to rise above.

_____

_____

_____

_____

_____

_____

_____

_____

_____

_____

_____

_____

_____

_____

_____

_____

Dear God, I celebrate you as the God of resurrection. There are dreams I have had and areas of my life that seem to have withered away and died long ago, but you have the power to help me bring them back to life. You will always bring new paths to walk, and your grace is always fresh and overflowing. Amen.

Dear _____ ,

MIDWEEK REFLECTION

How are things going for you this week, so far? What more can you do this week to focus your intentions and move forward on your path to a meaningful life?

_____

_____

_____

_____

_____

_____

_____

MY YIPPEE! MOMENT OF THE WEEK . . .

What brought you joy or made you smile this week?

_____

_____

_____

_____

_____

_____

_____

Give Up on Complaining

"True happiness comes not when we get rid of all of our problems, but when we change our relationship to them, when we see our problems as a potential source of awakening, opportunities to practice patience, and to learn."

—Richard Carlson

Sometimes, it can seem like there's a lot to complain about in life. Lord knows that I've done my fair share of complaining, but over time I've found something that helps. This week, try to focus your complaining to ten to fifteen minutes per day, max. Try to focus it during that one part of your day, then leave the rest of the day free. Write down what you have to complain about right here, right now, then work to take one thing off the list, or work on accepting what you can't change at the moment.

_____

_____

_____

_____

_____

_____

_____

_____

_____

_____

Dear God, please help me to stop complaining, to stop focusing on what's wrong, to stop zeroing in on what I regard as people's faults. Help me to focus instead on what's beautiful in my life and the gifts that have been given to me. Give me the grace to forgive others quickly and completely and to move forward in my life. Amen.

Dear _____ ,

MIDWEEK REFLECTION

How are things going for you this week, so far? What more can you do this week to focus your intentions and move forward on your path to a meaningful life?

_____

_____

_____

_____

_____

_____

_____

MY YIPPEE! MOMENT OF THE WEEK . . .

What brought you joy or made you smile this week?

_____

_____

_____

_____

_____

_____

Moving On

"Do it well, finish it properly, and move on."

—Eunice Kennedy Shriver

Moving on. It's one of those phrases that's way easier for us to say than actually do. If you're trying to "move on" from something right now, be gentle with yourself. Know that moving on takes time. This week, use this space to write down what you want to move on from and to visualize what moving on looks like and feels like to you. Remember, only move on when you're ready—not when someone else tries to tell you to do it.

_____

_____

_____

_____

_____

_____

_____

_____

_____

_____

_____

_____

_____

_____

_____

_____

_____

Dear God, when I look ahead, the future seems scary and leaves me feeling very vulnerable and insecure. When I don't know what is going to happen, remind me that you know the plans you have for me and that you are directing my steps. I look forward with confidence to your leading me into a bright tomorrow. Amen.

Dear _____ ,

MIDWEEK REFLECTION

How are things going for you this week, so far? What more can you do this week to focus your intentions and move forward on your path to a meaningful life?

_____

_____

_____

_____

_____

_____

MY YIPPEE! MOMENT OF THE WEEK . . .

What brought you joy or made you smile this week?

_____

_____

_____

_____

_____

_____

WEEK 20

Loving Motherhood

"Motherhood is one of those jobs that you do every day. It never stops and you're never done. You work 24/7, 365 days a year—for your entire life."

—Maria

Motherhood, in my opinion, is the most powerful job on earth. To mother is to nurture, to listen, to show up, to care, and to be there for another person. It means to be all in, and then to step back out. Over time, I've also come to realize that there are a lot of really good mothers out there who have never even given birth. That's because we all have the ability to mother, whether we have children or not. This week, use this space to write down how you mother the people in your life. What do you like about your role? How do you describe your role? How might you do it better? Also use this space to think about those who have mothered you.

_____

_____

_____

_____

_____

_____

_____

_____

_____

_____

_____

Dear God, help me to always remember that the most important job I have on earth is to mother. People need mothering at all times in their lives, so use me as a channel to nurture and love those who need it most. Amen.

Dear _____ ,

MIDWEEK REFLECTION

How are things going for you this week, so far? What more can you do this week to focus your intentions and move forward on your path to a meaningful life?

_____

_____

_____

_____

_____

_____

_____

MY YIPPEE! MOMENT OF THE WEEK . . .

What brought you joy or made you smile this week?

_____

_____

_____

_____

_____

_____

A Message from My Mother I Will Cherish Forever

"To Maria, Only in Heaven will I love you more."

—Eunice Kennedy Shriver

One day when I was tidying up my home, I came across a book inscribed to me by my mother. It included the quote above, and upon reading it I immediately burst into tears because I knew its words were true. It was a message I didn't know even existed, but it was one that I needed to hear in that very moment. It's now a message that I will cherish in my heart forever. What is a message that you've received that has deeply affected your life and touched your heart forever? What might you write as a message in a book to someone you love? (After all, you never know when they might open it, read it, and need it.)

_____

_____

_____

_____

_____

_____

_____

_____

_____

_____

_____

_____

_____

Dear God, thank you for the unexpected gifts of love that are all around me. May I continue to stay open to finding them, seeing them, and letting them into my heart. Amen.

Dear_____ ,

MIDWEEK REFLECTION

How are things going for you this week, so far? What more can you do this week to focus your intentions and move forward on your path to a meaningful life?

_____

_____

_____

_____

_____

_____

_____

MY YIPPEE! MOMENT OF THE WEEK . . .

What brought you joy or made you smile this week?

_____

_____

_____

_____

_____

_____

_____

Finding Peace in Your Decisions

> "Life is full of tough decisions, and nothing makes
> them easy. . . . Try, trust, try, and trust again, and
> eventually you'll feel your mind change its focus
> to a new level of understanding."
>
> —Martha Beck

We all struggle with indecision at one point or another in our lives. I know I have. The process of deciding and being at peace with our decisions requires faith in ourselves to know what's right. What tough decision are you facing right now? How can you trust yourself to find your way? (If you're really struggling, I recommend you look up the Ignatian Framework for Discernment. It will walk you through the decision-making process and, I hope, make it a bit easier for you.) Remember, a decision is just that: one decision. You can always decide to make a new decision at any time.

_____

_____

_____

_____

_____

_____

_____

_____

_____

_____

Dear God, I struggle with making decisions. I worry that I will make the wrong ones, so I get paralyzed and make no decisions at all. Please help me change this. Please help me take the action of making my decision and leaving the results to you. I know that no matter what happens, you will help me. Amen.

Dear _____ ,

MIDWEEK REFLECTION

How are things going for you this week, so far? What more can you do this week to focus your intentions and move forward on your path to a meaningful life?

_____

_____

_____

_____

_____

_____

_____

MY YIPPEE! MOMENT OF THE WEEK . . .

What brought you joy or made you smile this week?

_____

_____

_____

_____

_____

_____

_____

The Power of Your Voice

"Change from within. To do that, you have to know yourself. You must look within and know what's right for you. You have to be capable of drowning out the other voices and listen to your own."

—Maria

You have your own distinct voice that's uniquely your own. It's super important to know how to use it, and when and where to use it. Do you recognize your voice? How are you using it? If you don't feel that you are, what's keeping you from speaking up? What's preventing you from being heard—be it at home, in the workplace, or in the world? Your voice is important, so get to know it. If it feels like work, know that writing will give your voice strength.

_____

_____

_____

_____

_____

_____

_____

_____

_____

_____

_____

_____

_____

_____

> *Dear God, help me to stop and listen to myself and have faith in the worthiness of my own voice. Help me to step away from the noise today, take a deep breath, quiet my heart and mind, and trust that you will help me hear what I need to hear. Amen.*

*Dear*_____ ,

MIDWEEK REFLECTION

How are things going for you this week, so far? What more can you do this week to focus your intentions and move forward on your path to a meaningful life?

_____

_____

_____

_____

_____

_____

MY YIPPEE! MOMENT OF THE WEEK . . .

What brought you joy or made you smile this week?

_____

_____

_____

_____

_____

_____

The Power of Fear

"If you want to be brave, then you have to walk into your fear."

—Maria

We all have fear. (I know I do.) Fear can be a motivator for some, but it's also really paralyzing for a lot of people. This week, write about your fears. What are you afraid of? How might you do more to push through your fear?

_____

_____

_____

_____

_____

_____

_____

_____

_____

_____

_____

_____

_____

_____

_____

_____

_____

_____

Dear God, please hold my hand when I'm feeling afraid and help me feel your strong and calming presence. I know that there is light on the other side of fear, even if it's hard to feel it in that moment. Help me know that you'll be standing with me on the other side. Amen.

Dear_____ ,

MIDWEEK REFLECTION

How are things going for you this week, so far? What more can you do this week to focus your intentions and move forward on your path to a meaningful life?

_____

_____

_____

_____

_____

_____

_____

MY YIPPEE! MOMENT OF THE WEEK . . .

What brought you joy or made you smile this week?

_____

_____

_____

_____

_____

_____

Men and Kindness

"Love and kindness are never wasted. They always make a difference. They bless the one who receives them, and they bless you, the giver."

—Barbara De Angelis

I've always tried to create a safe space for those whom I love. I've also tried to teach my children (my two boys and my two girls) that being vulnerable and honest with their emotions is a sign of strength. This week, think about the men in your life, in particular, and how you can create a safe space for them to express their emotions. After all, that's something many men find difficult to do. How can you foster their expression? What can you do to accept their emotions?

_____

_____

_____

_____

_____

_____

_____

_____

_____

_____

_____

_____

_____

_____

> *Build me a son, O Lord, whose heart will be clear, whose goal will be high; a son who will master himself before he seeks to master other men; one who will reach into the future, yet never forget the past. . . . Give him humility, so that he may always remember the simplicity of true greatness, the open mind of true wisdom, and the weakness of true strength.*
> *—General Douglas MacArthur*

Dear_____,

MIDWEEK REFLECTION

How are things going for you this week, so far? What more can you do this week to focus your intentions and move forward on your path to a meaningful life?

_____

_____

_____

_____

_____

_____

_____

MY YIPPEE! MOMENT OF THE WEEK . . .

What brought you joy or made you smile this week?

_____

_____

_____

_____

_____

_____

_____

MIDYEAR CHECK-IN

It's hard to believe we're already halfway through the year. How are you feeling about your year so far? Take a moment to flip back to the beginning of your journal and reflect on the intentions you set for yourself when you started. Are you walking the path you hoped you would be? What roadblocks have been thrown at you along the way? How can you reset your intentions, if needed, and continue to find the strength to live a life of intention and purpose in the months ahead?

The Power of Service

"One person can make a difference, and everyone should try."

—President John F. Kennedy

As my uncle once stated, we all have the power to make a difference in the world. You don't have to be someone powerful or famous to have great influence, or to be of service in the lives of others. This country was built by people who gave their lives and it's still being made better all the time by those who give of themselves. This week, think about how you can be of service. Are you giving back? If not, think about what's keeping you from doing it (and don't tell me you don't have time).

_____

_____

_____

_____

_____

_____

_____

_____

_____

_____

Dear God, help me to see myself as a beacon of light in this world. Help me to recognize the unique talents and strengths that I possess and that I can use to better the lives of others, including myself. Amen.

Dear _____ ,

MIDWEEK REFLECTION

How are things going for you this week, so far? What more can you do this week to focus your intentions and move forward on your path to a meaningful life?

_____

_____

_____

_____

_____

_____

_____

MY YIPPEE! MOMENT OF THE WEEK . . .

What brought you joy or made you smile this week?

_____

_____

_____

_____

_____

_____

We're All in This Together

"All of our humanity is dependent upon recognizing the humanity in others."

—Archbishop Desmond Tutu

I am connected to you, and you are connected to me. We share the same planet. We breathe the same air. Our future depends on seeing our common humanity. This week, I ask you to take a moment to think about how we can do a better job of connecting and coming together. How can you see the shared humanity in those around you? Also, what does freedom mean to you, and how can you help others also feel free?

_____

_____

_____

_____

_____

_____

_____

_____

_____

_____

_____

_____

_____

_____

_____

_____

_____

> *Dear God, help me to remember that I am part of a larger humanity. Please help me remember that what is good for me is good for others. Help me not to judge others, but to treat them with acceptance and compassion. Help us all to treat our common home—the planet earth—with the same love and care. Amen.*

Dear _____ ,

MIDWEEK REFLECTION

How are things going for you this week, so far? What more can you do this week to focus your intentions and move forward on your path to a meaningful life?

_____

_____

_____

_____

_____

_____

_____

MY YIPPEE! MOMENT OF THE WEEK . . .

What brought you joy or made you smile this week?

_____

_____

_____

_____

_____

_____

Something to Focus on Other Than Your Lips, Thighs, and Eyes

"It's beyond mind-blowing to find yourself sitting across from a parent who has Alzheimer's and has no idea who you are, or worse, who they are."

—Maria

Every sixty-five seconds in this country, a new brain develops Alzheimer's disease. Two-thirds of those brains belong to women, and no one knows why that is. After Alzheimer's robbed my father of his brilliant mind, I became determined to seek answers and advocate on behalf of the millions of other families who are struggling with this disease. This week, I want you to think about your own precious brainpower and how you can care for it. How can you incorporate more sleep, healthy eating, exercise, and meditation into your daily routine? I know these things aren't always easy, but I strongly believe that we should all try.

_____

_____

_____

_____

_____

_____

_____

_____

_____

_____

_____

Dear God, please guide me toward better health, to eat well, to exercise well, to learn more, and to be social as well. Hold my life in your hands and renew my mind, body, soul, and spirit. With you, all things are possible. Amen.

Dear _____ ,

MIDWEEK REFLECTION

How are things going for you this week, so far? What more can you do this week to focus your intentions and move forward on your path to a meaningful life?

_____

_____

_____

_____

_____

_____

_____

MY YIPPEE! MOMENT OF THE WEEK . . .

What brought you joy or made you smile this week?

_____

_____

_____

_____

_____

_____

_____

Working on "Intestinal Fortitude"

"Failure isn't fatal, but failure to change might be."

—John Wooden

Our true power—our true strength—lies within us. I like to call it our "intestinal fortitude," and how we use it determines how well we respond to the challenges that life throws us. This week, reflect on a time in your life when you tapped into your inner strength to respond to a difficult person or situation. Are you proud of how you handled that moment? Do you believe that you have intestinal fortitude? I bet you have more than you realize . . .

_____

_____

_____

_____

_____

_____

_____

_____

_____

_____

_____

_____

_____

_____

_____

*Dear God, help me speak from a place of calm, loving strength.
Help me speak with positive intention, not with the intention of
demeaning or diminishing another. Help me to find the right
words to do that, the right thoughts, the right tone. Help me to
speak without fear. Help me to speak the truth with grace and
lovingkindness. Amen.*

Dear _____ ,

MIDWEEK REFLECTION

How are things going for you this week, so far? What more can you do this week to focus your intentions and move forward on your path to a meaningful life?

_____

_____

_____

_____

_____

_____

_____

MY YIPPEE! MOMENT OF THE WEEK . . .

What brought you joy or made you smile this week?

_____

_____

_____

_____

_____

_____

_____

Chasing the Illusion of Perfection

"I see the good in me and in others. I see the love in me and in others. I see the imperfection in me and in others, and I look at it with compassion and understanding."

—Maria

Believe me, nobody is perfect, and there is no such thing as a perfect life. A meaningful life, in fact, is full of imperfections. It's full of ups and downs, mistakes and amends, the good and the bad, the dark and the light. This I know for sure. Long ago, I gave up trying to live a perfect life because I realized that it's impossible. That's why focusing on living a meaningful life is so much better—it feels attainable. This week, think about an area of your life where you might be aiming a little too hard for perfection. Can you let that go? How could you be gentler with yourself? How can you focus more on what will bring you meaning and make you feel good? Lose the perfect. Aim for the good.

_____

_____

_____

_____

_____

_____

_____

_____

_____

> *Dear God, please help me to let go of trying to be perfect. Help me to realize that I am okay as I am. I was born sacred, and I will always be sacred. Help me to remember that when I stay focused on comparing myself to others—or to some illusion of perfection—I always come up short, and that's not honoring the gift of life you've given me. Help me to remember I am one of your precious children, and I am enough. Amen.*

Dear _____ ,

MIDWEEK REFLECTION

How are things going for you this week, so far? What more can you do this week to focus your intentions and move forward on your path to a meaningful life?

_____

_____

_____

_____

_____

_____

_____

MY YIPPEE! MOMENT OF THE WEEK . . .

What brought you joy or made you smile this week?

_____

_____

_____

_____

_____

_____

Why Acceptance Is the Path to Finding Peace

"If we have no peace, it is because we have forgotten that we belong to each other."

—Saint Teresa of Calcutta

At the end of the day, we all want to belong. We all want to be accepted. Recognizing that we share this common desire can help us see our shared humanity. This week, ask yourself: Do I accept myself as I am? (If you're like me, you've probably struggled with parts of yourself at one point or another. That's okay.) Focus on accepting yourself— your whole self—right now. Then, focus on how you can accept others as well. Accepting others and accepting yourself will help you on your path to peace.

_____

_____

_____

_____

_____

_____

_____

_____

_____

_____

_____

_____

_____

_____

_____

Dear God, help me to accept others the same way you accept me. Empower me to accept people who are different and especially those who often experience rejection and are made to feel unacceptable. I want to love others as you have loved me. Amen.

Dear _____ ,

MIDWEEK REFLECTION

How are things going for you this week, so far? What more can you do this week to focus your intentions and move forward on your path to a meaningful life?

_____

_____

_____

_____

_____

_____

_____

MY YIPPEE! MOMENT OF THE WEEK . . .

What brought you joy or made you smile this week?

_____

_____

_____

_____

_____

_____

Why It Takes Courage to Care

"Many see care as soft, but it's anything but. It takes courage to care. It takes passion to stand up for someone or something you believe in and care about."

—Maria

I think a lot about care—the word, the concept, the act of caring. I've been thinking about how I define care, and about how vital caring is to a healthy family, a healthy community, and a healthy country. This week, try to think about how you define care. How do you care for yourself and those around you? Do the people you're caring for even know you're doing it? Ask people you love how they define care. Ask them about their "care language." Remember, to care is an act of love.

_____

_____

_____

_____

_____

_____

_____

_____

_____

_____

_____

_____

_____

Dear God, thank you for caring about me and for me. And thank you for allowing me to feel cared for by others. We have been told, "Blessed are the peacemakers," but may I also remember that "Blessed are the caregivers, too." Remind me not to overlook the simple but powerful act of caring. Let me be aware when people extend their caring to me, and may I extend it to others. Amen.

Dear _____ ,

MIDWEEK REFLECTION

How are things going for you this week, so far? What more can you do this week to focus your intentions and move forward on your path to a meaningful life?

_____

_____

_____

_____

_____

_____

_____

MY YIPPEE! MOMENT OF THE WEEK . . .

What brought you joy or made you smile this week?

_____

_____

_____

_____

_____

_____

_____

Time: Your Most Precious Asset

"Get living. Don't wait until your back is up against the wall to dance, to gather, to be kind, to say what needs to be said, or to ask someone to hold your hand."

—Maria

Our lives throw a lot at us day after day. That's why it's so important for us to take a beat and ask ourselves whether we're using our time to set priorities that matter most to us. Do you make time for yourself? Time for your friends? Time for your family? Time to live? Or are you too busy? How might you make more time for what you value? One thing I've found helpful is to draw a picture of a pie, then write down all the people and things that are getting a piece of my time. Try doing the same yourself. How is your pie divided? Are you spending the time where you think you are?

_____

_____

_____

_____

_____

_____

_____

_____

_____

_____

_____

_____

> *Dear God, thank you for the time you have given me on this precious earth. Thank you for my health and my ability to enjoy the time I spend here. May I always appreciate the moments of every day and never take one that you have given me for granted. Amen.*

Dear _____ ,

MIDWEEK REFLECTION

How are things going for you this week, so far? What more can you do this week to focus your intentions and move forward on your path to a meaningful life?

_____

_____

_____

_____

_____

_____

_____

MY YIPPEE! MOMENT OF THE WEEK . . .

What brought you joy or made you smile this week?

_____

_____

_____

_____

_____

_____

_____

I've Learned to Deserve

"If you look at what you have in life, you'll always have more. If you look at what you don't have in life, you'll never have enough."

—Oprah Winfrey

I love that quote from my friend Oprah because it always reminds me to appreciate my life exactly as it is, and to know that I deserve all the blessings I have received in my life. Look at your life today and all that you have. Look at the good—not at what's missing. Write down a list of what you believe you deserve, because trust me, you do deserve it. Don't use this space this week to write down anything negative. (If you have a complaint, go back to the complaint page!) This page is for what you deserve.

_____

_____

_____

_____

_____

_____

_____

_____

_____

_____

_____

_____

_____

_____

_____

_____

_____

> *Dear God, you've given me so many gifts. Help me to know that*
> *I deserve them. Help me to know that you love me deeply and*
> *that I deserve that love. Amen.*

Dear _____ ,

MIDWEEK REFLECTION

How are things going for you this week, so far? What more can you do this week to focus your intentions and move forward on your path to a meaningful life?

_____

_____

_____

_____

_____

_____

_____

MY YIPPEE! MOMENT OF THE WEEK . . .

What brought you joy or made you smile this week?

_____

_____

_____

_____

_____

_____

_____

When Life Throws You a Curveball, Do This

"You have to go internal if you want to go eternal."

—Sargent Shriver

Life throws all of us curveballs at one time or another. I don't care who you are or how much money you have—a curveball is going to come your way. How you navigate the curveballs has a lot to do with what you believe in and whether you believe in yourself. My father said the words above when he was deep in Alzheimer's, and his wisdom has stayed with me ever since. When life throws me a curveball, I go internal, gather myself, and then move forward. Where do you go when life throws you a curveball?

_____

_____

_____

_____

_____

_____

_____

_____

_____

_____

_____

_____

_____

_____

_____

_____

Dear God, when I feel confused or uncertain about the direction I should take or how I should deal with a situation or person, help me to find wise counsel. Please help me listen for your wisdom, and lead me to those through whom you speak, who can wisely discern what is right for me. Amen.

Dear _____ ,

MIDWEEK REFLECTION

How are things going for you this week, so far? What more can you do this week to focus your intentions and move forward on your path to a meaningful life?

_____

_____

_____

_____

_____

_____

_____

MY YIPPEE! MOMENT OF THE WEEK . . .

What brought you joy or made you smile this week?

_____

_____

_____

_____

_____

_____

_____

Take Time to Rest

"Each day, each of us is faced with the possibility
of resetting our lives. Refocusing. Reimagining.
Rebooting. Every day, we can decide to change
our outlook, our words, our tone, our attitude."

—Maria

In the hustle and bustle of life, take a beat to gather yourself, refocus, and recharge. After all, I believe that rest is essential if we want to reflect on who we are and why we do what we do. Do you make time for rest, or do you judge those who rest? Do you recharge? If you don't, then take it from me: resting is imperative to your health and your thoughts.

_____

_____

_____

_____

_____

_____

_____

_____

*Dear God, it feels as though the world is coming apart at the
seams, and my world of constant motion is spinning with stress.
You taught us that you wanted us to slow down sometimes and
get rest for body and soul and mind and spirit, to recharge our
batteries and refocus our resolve. Help me to stop and reflect on
what I'm doing, and why I'm doing it, and to know my purpose
and mission in this life. Help me to be still and know that you
are God and to hear you speak, so that I can move forward with
strength and confidence. Amen.*

Dear _____ ,

MIDWEEK REFLECTION

How are things going for you this week, so far? What more can you do this week to focus your intentions and move forward on your path to a meaningful life?

_____

_____

_____

_____

_____

_____

_____

MY YIPPEE! MOMENT OF THE WEEK . . .

What brought you joy or made you smile this week?

_____

_____

_____

_____

_____

_____

WEEK 37

The Power of Empathy

"The best and most beautiful things in the world cannot be seen or even touched, but must be felt with the heart."

—Helen Keller

Empathy is a feeling. It's the ability to share someone else's feelings or to understand their experiences. Some people are born with empathy, while others need to work at cultivating it. Today, think about a time when someone expressed empathy for you. What did that feel like? What did it mean to you? How have you expressed empathy for someone else? Empathy is a critical life skill, so learn how to stand in someone else's shoes. Believe me, you'll need someone to stand in yours at some point in life. (And if you're low on the empathy meter, make it a yearly goal to get it higher.)

_____

_____

_____

_____

_____

_____

_____

_____

_____

_____

_____

_____

_____

_____

_____

Dear God, please give me the gift of empathy, of understanding another person's life experiences. Help me to listen to those experiences without judgment. Soften my heart, so that I may feel the heart of another. Amen.

Dear _____ ,

MIDWEEK REFLECTION

How are things going for you this week, so far? What more can you do this week to focus your intentions and move forward on your path to a meaningful life?

_____

_____

_____

_____

_____

_____

_____

MY YIPPEE! MOMENT OF THE WEEK . . .

What brought you joy or made you smile this week?

_____

_____

_____

_____

_____

_____

_____

The Power of Letting Go

"Some people believe holding on and hanging in there are great signs of strength. However, there are times when it takes much more strength to know when to let go and then do it."

—Ann Landers

Letting go can be hard. It can be hard to let go of limiting beliefs, of stories you tell yourself, of people, or of the way things are. This week, use this space to write down what beliefs you have that no longer serve you. Write down what you need to let go of now. Do you struggle with letting go? If so, why?

_____

_____

_____

_____

_____

_____

_____

_____

_____

_____

_____

_____

_____

_____

_____

_____

_____

> *Dear God, letting go is hard for me, because I want to hold on and be in control. That makes me feel safe. Help me to realize that I am safe, even when I let go of the way things are and allow them to unfold in the new ways they're supposed to. Amen.*

Dear _____ ,

MIDWEEK REFLECTION

How are things going for you this week, so far? What more can you do this week to focus your intentions and move forward on your path to a meaningful life?

MY YIPPEE! MOMENT OF THE WEEK . . .

What brought you joy or made you smile this week?

The Power of Boundaries

"So many of us are better at protecting others than ourselves. Today, take your warrior self and apply it to you. Don't let anyone come at your spirit, at your light, at your know-how, or at your truth. Protect yourself because you are worthy of the protection you offer to others."

—Maria

I first heard about the concept of "boundaries" when I was in my fifties. I'm late to the game, but I've come to learn that boundaries are important at every stage in life, especially if you want to have your own life. Setting boundaries is never easy, especially with those you love. But remember, boundaries aren't selfish or mean. They're acts of self-care. So, this week, use this space to write down what healthy boundaries mean to you and where you might set some boundaries in your life.

_____

_____

_____

_____

_____

_____

_____

_____

_____

_____

_____

_____

_____

_____

_____

> _Dear God, please help me to establish boundaries. Please help me teach people how I want to be treated. Please also help the people I love know that my boundaries don't mean I love them any less. Amen._

Dear _____ ,

MIDWEEK REFLECTION

How are things going for you this week, so far? What more can you do this week to focus your intentions and move forward on your path to a meaningful life?

_____

_____

_____

_____

_____

_____

_____

MY YIPPEE! MOMENT OF THE WEEK . . .

What brought you joy or made you smile this week?

_____

_____

_____

_____

_____

_____

_____

WEEK 40

The Power of Faith

"Do not go where the path may lead. Go instead where there is no path and leave a trail."

—attributed to Ralph Waldo Emerson

If you want to forge your own path in life, if you want to live a life that's uniquely your own, then you're going to need to have a lot of faith in yourself. How do you define faith? Do you believe that you actually have faith in yourself? Do you believe in yourself? If not, how can you build more self-esteem and more faith in yourself? Write down one or two things that come to mind.

_____

_____

_____

_____

_____

_____

_____

_____

_____

_____

_____

_____

_____

_____

_____

_____

_____

> *Dear God, I acknowledge that in myself I am weak and vulnerable, but I rejoice that you are on my side and that I am no one's victim. Thank you for being strong in my life. Thank you for letting nothing, no matter how painful or powerful, separate me from your love. That makes me victorious, no matter what. Amen.*

Dear _____ ,

MIDWEEK REFLECTION

How are things going for you this week, so far? What more can you do this week to focus your intentions and move forward on your path to a meaningful life?

MY YIPPEE! MOMENT OF THE WEEK . . .

What brought you joy or made you smile this week?

The Power of Prayer
and Meditation

"Prayer is talking to God. Meditation is letting
God talk to you."

—Yogi Bhajan

Every morning, I try to start my day in stillness. I pray, I reflect, I meditate. I ask for guidance, and I wait for the answer. (I've been waiting for some answers for quite some time.) This week, use this space to write down what kind of guidance you're looking for. Do you know where you want to go? Who or what might help you get there? If you don't know, then pray, meditate, and seek guidance. Wait for the answer.

_____

_____

_____

_____

_____

_____

_____

_____

_____

_____

_____

_____

_____

_____

_____

_____

> *Dear God, may I spend time with you every day, quieting the cares and concerns that make so much noise in my mind, heart, and spirit, so that I can hear your wisdom and feel the love you've given me every day of my life. Amen.*

Dear_____ ,

MIDWEEK REFLECTION

How are things going for you this week, so far? What more can you do this week to focus your intentions and move forward on your path to a meaningful life?

_____

_____

_____

_____

_____

_____

MY YIPPEE! MOMENT OF THE WEEK . . .

What brought you joy or made you smile this week?

_____

_____

_____

_____

_____

_____

The Power of Forgiveness

"The weak can never forgive. Forgiveness is the attribute of the strong."

—Mahatma Gandhi

Forgiveness is a complicated process. It's also an ongoing process—one that can take some time. This week, use this space to write down your definition of forgiveness. Who would you like to forgive? What's holding you back? Be gentle with yourself here. Use this space to think about ways that you might forgive yourself. After all, sometimes we're not only mad at someone else, but we're also mad at ourselves.

_____

_____

_____

_____

_____

_____

_____

_____

_____

_____

_____

_____

_____

_____

_____

_____

_____

Dear God, *don't let me be caught in resentment or any other form of fear and hate. If they appear, please turn my thoughts into prayer for my enemy or someone in need.*
                                    —*Father Frank Desiderio, CSP*

Dear _____ ,

MIDWEEK REFLECTION

How are things going for you this week, so far? What more can you do this week to focus your intentions and move forward on your path to a meaningful life?

_____

_____

_____

_____

_____

_____

_____

MY YIPPEE! MOMENT OF THE WEEK . . .

What brought you joy or made you smile this week?

_____

_____

_____

_____

_____

_____

The Power of Your Story

"There is no greater agony than bearing an untold story inside you."

—Maya Angelou

A friend wisely told me once, "*You* are the hero of your own story." It's true. So, own the story of your life. Value it. Give yourself credit where it's due. This week, reflect on the story of your life and all the decisions you've made that have gotten you to where you are today. What are you most proud of? Where could you give yourself more credit? Can you see yourself as being on a hero's journey? (You are, so I recommend you start thinking of your life that way.)

_____

_____

_____

_____

_____

_____

Dear God, help me to tell my story with compassion for myself. Help me to be gentle with myself for the decisions I have made and will make. And help guide me to make good choices as my story continues to unfold. Amen.

Dear _____ ,

MIDWEEK REFLECTION

How are things going for you this week, so far? What more can you do this week to focus your intentions and move forward on your path to a meaningful life?

_____

_____

_____

_____

_____

_____

MY YIPPEE! MOMENT OF THE WEEK . . .

What brought you joy or made you smile this week?

_____

_____

_____

_____

_____

_____

The Power of You

"I have one life and one chance to make it count for something. . . . My faith demands that I do whatever I can, wherever I am, whenever I can, for as long as I can, with whatever I have, to try to make a difference."

—President Jimmy Carter

Y ou have the power to change your life. Think about that. You also have the power to make a huge impact on another person's life by the way you love them, see them, and care for them. Think about the impact you've had on someone else's life. Also think about who has made an impact on you. Have you thanked them? Use this space to think about that, and also to think about the kind of impact that you want to have on the world and on others.

_____

_____

_____

_____

_____

_____

_____

_____

_____

_____

_____

_____

_____

_____

_____

_____

Dear God, help me to confidently answer the call to help make the world a better place by being caring, tender, and respectful toward others. Help me to be the best version of the person you created me to be. Amen.

Dear _____ ,

MIDWEEK REFLECTION

How are things going for you this week, so far? What more can you do this week to focus your intentions and move forward on your path to a meaningful life?

_____

_____

_____

_____

_____

_____

MY YIPPEE! MOMENT OF THE WEEK . . .

What brought you joy or made you smile this week?

_____

_____

_____

_____

_____

_____

Life Is Yours to Create . . .
And to Re-create

"It's your road and yours alone. Others may walk
it with you, but no one can walk it for you."

—Rumi

There goes Rumi again, speaking the truth. Knowing that your life is yours and yours alone can be scary for some people, but it can also be very empowering. You are the captain of your own ship. You get to decide the terms of your life—who to bring into your life, and who to ask to leave it. And if your life isn't going in the way you want, you can change that. This week, write about how you're currently defining your own life. Do you like where you are? If you don't, please don't despair. Remember that you have the power to create and re-create.

_____

_____

_____

_____

_____

_____

_____

_____

_____

_____

_____

Dear God, you are the God of transformation. Help me to be brave. Help me to trust you and believe that I am here to write my life story in a way that brings glory to you and joy to myself and to others. Amen.

Dear _____ ,

MIDWEEK REFLECTION

How are things going for you this week, so far? What more can you do this week to focus your intentions and move forward on your path to a meaningful life?

_____

_____

_____

_____

_____

_____

MY YIPPEE! MOMENT OF THE WEEK . . .

What brought you joy or made you smile this week?

_____

_____

_____

_____

_____

_____

The Power of the Pause

"Realize deeply that the present moment is all you
ever have."

—Eckhart Tolle

This present moment is all you'll ever have, so right
now, take a deep breath. Pause and allow yourself to
feel exactly whatever you're feeling in this moment.
How can you do a better job of honoring what you feel, and allowing yourself to slow down and get in touch with your innermost self every day? This week, ask yourself how you might
check your intentions in each moment before you rush to move
forward and take action.

_____

_____

_____

_____

_____

_____

_____

_____

_____

_____

_____

_____

_____

_____

_____

Dear God, I need to slow my life down to see, really see, the people in my life. Help me to be so conscious of them that I take the time to look into their eyes and connect with the person who is right there in front of me. Amen.

Dear _____ ,

MIDWEEK REFLECTION

How are things going for you this week, so far? What more can you do this week to focus your intentions and move forward on your path to a meaningful life?

_____

_____

_____

_____

_____

_____

_____

MY YIPPEE! MOMENT OF THE WEEK . . .

What brought you joy or made you smile this week?

_____

_____

_____

_____

_____

_____

_____

What I'm Grateful for This Thanksgiving

"Sally, Thanksgiving is a very important holiday. Ours was the first country in the world to make a national holiday to give thanks."

—Charles M. Schulz

Thanksgiving is a holiday all about giving thanks, which is why it's my favorite holiday of the year. It's also a day when we're reminded of why we should be giving thanks each and every day of the year. This week, think about what you are most grateful for this year, so far. How can you extend your gratitude to those you love today, and every day?

_____

_____

_____

_____

_____

_____

_____

_____

_____

_____

_____

_____

_____

_____

_____

_____

_____

> *Dear God, thank you for the experience of finding delight in even the simplest things in life. Help me never to take what you've given me for granted. Thank you, thank you, thank you. Amen.*

Dear _____ ,

MIDWEEK REFLECTION

How are things going for you this week, so far? What more can you do this week to focus your intentions and move forward on your path to a meaningful life?

_____

_____

_____

_____

_____

_____

_____

MY YIPPEE! MOMENT OF THE WEEK . . .

What brought you joy or made you smile this week?

_____

_____

_____

_____

_____

_____

_____

Faith Keepers

"At certain points in life, the hill gets steeper, the climb more intense, the hope fades. But if we continue to work, to have faith, to believe . . . we will power through."

—Maria

No matter what challenges you're facing in your life right now, it helps to have a group of people around who have faith in you. I call this group of people my faith keepers and they help keep me on track. When the climb is intense, these people will climb with you. When you need someone to speak truth to you, these people will do it. Who are the faith keepers in your life? Write them down. If you don't have a group you trust, then start building your team. We all need a group of people that will be there for us in the good times and the bad.

_____

_____

_____

_____

_____

_____

_____

_____

_____

_____

_____

_____

_____

_____

_____

_____

Dear God, thank you for populating my life with the wonderful women and men who are my faith keepers. I know that you talk to me through them and love me through them and teach me through them and laugh with me through them. Amen.

Dear _____ ,

MIDWEEK REFLECTION

How are things going for you this week, so far? What more can you do this week to focus your intentions and move forward on your path to a meaningful life?

_____

_____

_____

_____

_____

_____

_____

MY YIPPEE! MOMENT OF THE WEEK . . .

What brought you joy or made you smile this week?

_____

_____

_____

_____

_____

_____

It's Okay—in Fact, It's Crucial—to Grieve

"Grief can surge back like a rogue wave, even when the person looks just fine on the outside."

—Kelly Buckley

Grief is something we all experience in life, but that we rarely ever discuss. I'm a big believer that it's important to talk about grief, write about grief, and express your grief. I'm mentioning this now as we're in the holiday season because I know some people find themselves sad at this time of year. But the truth is that grief can come up at many points in our lives. So today, write about your feelings and any grief you may be feeling. Don't be afraid of your sadness or your grief. Also ask yourself, do I have someone to share my grief with? If not, where can I turn? (Whether you have someone or not, know that there are a lot of professionals out there who can help with grief.)

_____

_____

_____

_____

_____

_____

_____

_____

_____

_____

Dear God, I trust you to help me face the unpredictable challenges and storms in my life. I choose to put my eyes on you and remember that you have promised to be with me, no matter what. I know that courage doesn't come just from confidence in my own strength, but from confidence in you. Thank you for the courage to face whatever lies ahead. Amen.

Dear _____ *,*

MIDWEEK REFLECTION

How are things going for you this week, so far? What more can you do this week to focus your intentions and move forward on your path to a meaningful life?

_____

_____

_____

_____

_____

_____

MY YIPPEE! MOMENT OF THE WEEK . . .

What brought you joy or made you smile this week?

_____

_____

_____

_____

_____

_____

_____

WEEK 50

The Holiday Season

"They say a person needs just three things to be truly happy in this world: someone to love, something to do, and something to hope for."

—Tom Bodett

The holiday season is a time when we often get swept up in the madness of buying gifts for others and receiving them ourselves. But this season, I encourage you to also take time to reflect on the gifts you have in your life already. What gifts has this past year given you? (And I'm not talking material gifts.) How can you give thanks to those who helped you receive them?

_____

_____

_____

_____

_____

_____

_____

_____

_____

_____

_____

_____

_____

_____

_____

_____

Dear God, please help me to see my life as a blessing and take the time to honor all that you have given me. Although I am always seeking to grow and get more from life, help me know that what you have given me is enough already. Amen.

Dear _____ ,

MIDWEEK REFLECTION

How are things going for you this week, so far? What more can you do this week to focus your intentions and move forward on your path to a meaningful life?

_____

_____

_____

_____

_____

_____

_____

MY YIPPEE! MOMENT OF THE WEEK . . .

What brought you joy or made you smile this week?

_____

_____

_____

_____

_____

_____

_____

The Power of Visualization

"The most fundamental aggression to ourselves, the most fundamental harm we can do to ourselves, is to remain ignorant by not having the courage and the respect to look at ourselves honestly and gently."

—Pema Chödrön

So many people want to make changes in their lives, and yet they find it difficult to do so. Visualization is a great technique that many athletes and business leaders use. That is, visualizing in your mind the life you want so that you can see clearly what it looks like and feels like. I myself have found visualization to be quite helpful in giving me direction on where I want to go. So today, visualize the life you want right now, as well as the one you want five or ten years from now. If you're struggling here, think about creating a vision board. Pull out pictures and quotes. Get quiet and just dream. If you're not quite where you want to be yet, remember that there's a whole new year on the horizon.

_____

_____

_____

_____

_____

_____

_____

_____

_____

_____

_____

> *Dear God, help me to see my full potential and to believe in my ability to reach it. I know that you believe in me and that I have what it takes to create the meaningful life I want. With each day forward, allow me to imagine the possibilities and take the actions I need to get there. Amen.*

Dear _____ ,

MIDWEEK REFLECTION

How are things going for you this week, so far? What more can you do this week to focus your intentions and move forward on your path to a meaningful life?

_____

_____

_____

_____

_____

_____

MY YIPPEE! MOMENT OF THE WEEK . . .

What brought you joy or made you smile this week?

_____

_____

_____

_____

_____

_____

WEEK 52

The Power of Reevaluating

"There comes a time in all of our lives when it's time to take stock of what was, what is, and what can be. Don't hold on to stuff that prevents you from becoming who you can be."

—Maria

Reevaluating your life can be painful, but it can also be incredibly liberating. As this year comes to a close, take a moment to evaluate all that you've learned over the last year. What were your challenges? What were your victories? What were you wrong about? (I've been wrong about a lot in my life.) How have you changed your mind? Remember, it's okay to change your mind.

_____

_____

_____

_____

_____

_____

_____

_____

_____

_____

_____

_____

_____

_____

_____

_____

> *Dear God, please guide me forward in my life. Help me to let go of beliefs and opinions that no longer serve me. Help me to drop critical judgments of myself and others. Remind me that I don't know other people's paths or pains. Help me to continue to grow into a more compassionate and caring human being—to others and to myself. Amen.*

Dear _____ ,

MIDWEEK REFLECTION

How are things going for you this week, so far? What more can you do this week to focus your intentions and move forward on your path to a meaningful life?

_____

_____

_____

_____

_____

_____

_____

MY YIPPEE! MOMENT OF THE WEEK . . .

What brought you joy or made you smile this week?

_____

_____

_____

_____

_____

_____

Oh! And One More Thing . . .

Before this year comes to a close, I want to take a minute to congratulate you for embarking on this journey.

Socrates said, "The unexamined life is not worth living." How true. You have been looking at yourself all year long. You've been working to dig in, let go, get better, be kinder, and become the passionate, divine person that you know you're capable of being. Bravo.

As you reflect on all that you've done and all that you've learned, I want to leave you with one other thing to do. One of the best things I've ever done in my life was start the tradition of Sunday family dinners. My family dinners enable me to grow, laugh, listen, learn, and share what I've learned and what I'm learning.

As you continue to move forward on this path to a meaningful life, make Sunday dinners a part of your weekly practice. Gather your family and friends around your table and expand your notion of what family means. Sunday dinners (or, really, dinner with loved ones any day of the week) are an opportunity to bring your beautiful self to the table. I'll bet people will marvel at who you are, all you have learned, and all you have to offer.

Draw your table below and write down who you want seated around it. Use pencil because every Sunday is a chance to grow and add to your table.

P.S. Remember to fill your plate (like your life) with healthy options. And always leave room for dessert!

Usually on the last page you put "The End," but there's no end to the path to a meaningful life. So, keep at it, and visit us at www.mariashriver.com/sundaypaper/ to tell us how it's going.

Acknowledgments

I love this journal, but I have to admit that it wasn't my idea.

It came from Lindsay Wilkes-Edrington, someone I work with every day. Lindsay told me how many people write in journals like this one and suggested that we create one as a companion to *I've Been Thinking* . . . .

This came to life because of her enthusiasm, determination, perseverance, and talent.

It also came to life with the support of my editor, Pam Dorman; the wonderful Brian Tart; the artistic genius of Nayon Cho, Claire Vaccaro, and Meighan Cavanaugh; and the organizational glue provided by Jeramie Orton. They are the team that believed in my book *I've Been Thinking* . . . . It was such a pleasure getting to work with them again on this journal and I am grateful to them all for their continued belief in me and my work.

I also want to extend much gratitude to Jan Miller and Shannon Marven. This is our ninth project together and I am so blessed to always have them by my side, believing in me and my voice.

Thank you, too, to my children for reading my work and encouraging me forward each and every day. I love you. Thank you to Patti Peterson for keeping me on track. Thank you to the team behind *The Sunday Paper* newsletter, which is where I publish my *I've Been Thinking . . .* columns each week.

And, finally, thank you to all of you—the readers, writers, and thinkers who bought *I've Been Thinking . . .* , who made it a #1 success, and who have now become ambassadors helping us promote *The Sunday Paper* as well. You are the ones this journal is for. You are the ones who came up to me and shared your stories and asked for a journal to house your own thoughts and reflections. This is for you. I hope you like the journal as much as I've enjoyed putting it together. I'll be thinking of you as you embark on this journey, writing your story on these pages, and living your one meaningful life. Have fun.

About the Author

Maria Shriver is the mother of four, a Peabody Award-winning and Emmy Award-winning journalist and producer, the author of seven *New York Times* bestselling books and a bestselling coloring book, an NBC News Special Anchor, and founder of The Women's Alzheimer's Movement. When she's not thinking or writing, she can be found hanging with her kids.